Stages of a Scattered Mess

A Broken Heart Poetry Collection

Poems of infatuation, love, and disillusion

To the Anacortes community,
   It has been an honor to call this beautiful place home. Thanks for the inspiration to continue my writing journey. Please help pass this book around within the community and leave a review on Goodreads and Amazon. Reviews help other readers find this poetry collection.

   — Author PAT

Stages of a Scattered Mess

PATRICK JOHNS

Stages of a Scattered Mess
Text copyright © 2021
Patrick Johns

Names, characters, organizations, places, and incidents are
either products of the author's imagination or are used
fictitiously and any resemblance to actual persons, living or
dead, business establishments, events, or locales is entirely
coincidental.

LCCN 2021914097
ISBN 978-0-9995268-3-5 (Paperback)
ISBN 978-0-9995268-2-8 (Hardback)

Cover image and book design by Patrick Johns

www.patrickjohnswrites.com

Special Thanks

To Jelena Vasic, for being the one who pushed me to share my words with the world.

To Mrs. Motto, my high school English teacher, for being the first to ever read one of my poems, and now, being the first to read my poetry book.

To Kalah McLaughlin, for helping me shape this poetry series.

To Kara Natchus, for her support in my words.

To Katie Herring, for teaching me it's all about the formatting.

To Laura Lucieri, for sharing her Photoshop knowledge.

To my family, for coping with my inner angst.

And to those who taught me how to love…

Thank you.

Preface

Stages of a Scattered Mess is the first installment of *A Broken Heart Poetry Collection*, focusing on poems of infatuation, love, and disillusion.

A Broken Heart Poetry Collection took me over a decade to write (2008 – 2020). During this time of teen angst and developing into a young adult, I wrote poems to help me cope with love, change, loss, pain, suffering, sacrifice, depression, failure, but more specifically—breakups. In summer 2018, I decided to go on a hunt for all of these poems. I had to dig through my old block phones, old computers, closets, and drawers. I collected everything I had and compiled all of it into a Word document. It was then when my heart began to ache as I realized I had to go through and read every single poem from the past twelve years. At that moment, I knew this was going to be difficult, knowing I would have to relive all of the memories of my teenage years and of my twenties.

A Broken Heart Poetry Collection will take you on the journey of the emotional struggles I went through while growing up (from the ages of 17 to 29). For me, growing up didn't start until I discovered what love was, how amazing love could be, and how much love could hurt when it's taken away. It was always the breakups in my life that made me discover myself just a little bit more. Who I am in this exact moment, blossomed from those breakups. If you had told the younger version of myself that I would be living in Spain and pursuing my dream of becoming a writer, I would have thought you were crazy. However, if it hadn't been for all the breakups, all the pain, all the failure I had experienced in my life, I would never have gotten the push I needed to pursue a better self.

My goal for this poetry collection is to help others who are currently suffering through emotional pain. Whether it's from a broken relationship, a lost loved one, a difficult change, pain is pain and don't let anyone tell you differently. We all experience pain in different ways.

But just know, on the other side of that pain, is a better, stronger you. Don't be afraid of pain. Don't be afraid of suffering. Don't be afraid to love again. Because the ones who succeed, grow, and learn in life are the ones who welcome failure and pain with open arms.

I want *A Broken Heart Poetry Collection* to be looked at not as a failure (from all the pain I had suffered), but as a success that has blossomed from that failure. Yes, I still carry these scars with me, and I always will for the rest of my life, but these scars are what have made me...

Me.

—Patrick Johns

I haven't been this scared
In a long time
And I'm so unprepared
So here's your valentine
Bouquet of clumsy words
A simple melody
This world's an ugly place
But you're so beautiful to me

—"Going Away to College" by Blink-182

Stage 1

Infatuation

No Lines Rehearsed

I have no lines rehearsed
Or no special quotes
Just my heart to spill
From my shaky voice
As I stand here like a fool
Taking in your beauty
Trying to find the words
To tell you how I feel

*First published by The Messenger Literary Magazine in October 2020.

The Mocking Pumpkin

A chill breeze
A campfire smell
A perfect day
But I nearly fell
As I stumbled to your door
I'm nervous
I can't tell
If you'll be there
When I knock
How long has it been
I check my watch
Only a second
Take a breath
She's probably upstairs
Getting dressed

A pumpkin sits
Right by your door
A face mocking me
From the floor
A grim smile
That never fades

Telling me to give up
   Walk
      Away

Was that a light
Or just the sun
Maybe I should give up
On our date
Let the pumpkin have its fun

It's late October
I'm at your door
I've never been
This nervous before

S o b e r

I feel like I'm drunk
But I've only had water
Staring at her eyes
Makes me want her
I'm falling

Falling so far

I feel like I'm drunk
But I've only had water

Sitting Next to You

The fire's burning
Up inside my head
The trees are no more
Can you see they're dead
But I am happy
This scene is lost
As long as you're here
You bring a happy thought
If it was up to me
I would hold you so close
But it's up to you
So what will you do
Make the right choice
There's no second shot
So if you want me here
Please speak up now

And if you want to know
The feelings inside
My heart will open
To you anytime
Make sure you're careful

And not too harsh
Because my feelings get hurt
Like any normal heart
Just know I will love you
Until the end
Your black hair
And your amazing trends
Get me every time
When I look at you
Never knowing
What's going to happen

And you're the only one
To fill my heart
Sick sad emotions
And now they're gone
Going to fill my dreams
With what I need
To reach the stars
I need you please
Sitting next to me
All along
You know I'm here
And we get along
The time is right
For you and I
To leave this place
All behind

Late Night at a Diner

Late night at a diner
I feel relaxed
Comfortable tonight
As you put your phone away
Listening to every word I say
You are different from all the rest
This is what my heart likes best
When you take my hand in yours
You look at me without any words
And I feel the love inside
Each and every time

In This Moment

It crosses my mind
How many guys
Were before my time
But it doesn't matter
Because in this moment
  She's kissing me

Take a Chance

I don't have the answers
I can't predict the future
All I can promise you is
You have my heart forever

Milky Way

Shooting past the stars
On this journey of ours
There goes the sun
And then there's Mars
Holding your hand
As we pass the moon
Through the Milky Way
We will be there soon

My heart beats fast
When you're in my sight
Just like traveling
At the speed of light
The Milky Way is big
For just us two
But just not enough
For my love for you

Falling For You

Let's hold hands
Jump off this world
And maybe we'll land
On someplace better
But I don't care where we are
As long as I'm in your arms
I'll fall with you forever
As long
   as we're together

I'll fall forever

Let's Rearrange

Let's rearrange
All the colors of the rainbow
To make a beautiful scene
A certain shade of blue
And your perfect green
We have control
Over anything and everything
Of all the surrounding scenery
When I'm with you
There's no limit to creativity
We can paint that house
On the beach we had dreamed
We can paint the sky tonight
And make the moon glow
As the stars burn bright
We can dance under it all
And gaze up as we fall
I'll catch you in our beautiful scene
Of my certain shade of blue
And your perfect green

H . E . R .

She's honestly everything I really need
Honestly everything I really care for
Everything I really love
Really all I desire

O p e n   S k y

Underneath the open sky
Your lips so close to mine
The smell of your perfume
Incorporating my mind
Deep into your loving eyes
I don't hesitate to take a dive
Stay in them past the night
As we shine in the moonlight

Our Favorite Colors

Blue
Is everything I see
When I look at you
Those perfect eyes
Delicately matching the sky
They make me want to fly
To discover something new with you

Red
The Taylor Swift poster
Hanging above your bed
As I hold you in my arms
Your head upon my chest
Watching you fall asleep
And slowly start to dream

October

Cold air
Fair skin
Rubbing against me again
As we watch the stars above
Cold breeze
Night-time
This is the reason why
October is the month of love

Green leaves fade away
Turn into a colored display
Bringing in a new year
A fresh page
Time for the weather to change
With brown eyes
A blue sky
Caught up in my mind
Reminding me the reason why
October is the month of love

Love This Summer

I told myself
I'd stay away
But everything fell into place
A look deep inside her eyes
Took me by surprise
Nothing I could do
But keep away
How could I when I felt this way
I told myself not this time
But faith seemed to feel otherwise

I never thought
It would come to this
A random night
With a random kiss
Brought me so far from this world
Making me fall so hard
For this girl

A simple night
Turned the chains
Blew me up

Spinning me away
I thought all of this
Would be just for fun
But it somehow turned
Deep into love

I didn't mean
To fall in love this summer
It took me by surprise
When I looked in her eyes
Under the stars
On the beach that night

S u m m e r

I know when it's summer
When the sun finally wakes up
And we start where we left off
The love which was put off
From going separate ways
But now the days grow longer
The feeling becomes stronger
As our hearts start to pound
With the love that surrounds us
It's been such a long year
But now you're finally here

I r e n a

When your friend, Irena, said
Get up, you guys are cute
Let me take a picture of you

I took you in my arms
You wore that dress
The one I really like

Behind us
We had some incredible views
Of mountains painted on blue

And in that moment
That summer fling
Sparked into something

When your friend, Irena, came with us
To go for a run
I thought we were only friends

I didn't have a clue
She'd be the one

22

Who'd push you right to me

It was her perfect plan
One I'd thank her about
After I took your hand

Who would have thought
This summer fling
Would turn into something

When your friend, Irena, was there
When you were scared
Before our first date

You had a message
In your hand
To cancel all our plans

But your friend, Irena, convinced you
No, don't send it
You need to go

And that night
This summer fling
Sparked into something

Boardwalk Stars

I want to spend my last night
Underneath these boardwalk stars
As our parents try to call
Wondering where we are
Let's cruise this Jersey line
One last night
And hope that somehow
It brings back the time

I want to sit on the beach
And gaze at the horizon
Watch the sunset
Hit the sea
Like a million diamonds
As far as the eye can see

I want to dance as the band
Plays their songs
On the stage underneath
These boardwalk stars
Holding your hand
As the night goes on

With the feeling
Nothing can go wrong
Tonight

So let's spend our last night
On all these rides
Sit on the beach
And wait for the tide
To reach our feet
And say goodbye
Holding you and
Staring into your eyes
All night long

Let's forget life
Just for a second
Tonight
So we can enjoy
These boardwalk stars
Just for tonight
We'll remember who we are

One last chance
One last time
Run to the edge of the line

Let's do it for real this time
Cross it

Never look back
Leave it all behind

We'll cruise this Jersey line
One last night
And we'll run
To the edge of the line

But until then
Let's enjoy
And never forget
All of these boardwalk stars

*First published by Ink & Sword Literary Magazine in February 2019.

Star Wars

Let's travel to a new planet
Be in our own Star Wars film
Because the gravity on Earth
Just isn't strong enough
I want to be closer to you
Where the days are long
And the nights even longer
Holding you in the sand
Where we can be in the endless suns
I'll be your Jedi Knight
Who saves you from the Sith lords
Because the action on Earth
Has no thrill
So let's travel a long
Long time ago
And live our Star Wars film

Let's Paint

Let's paint your eyes
Let's paint your bed
All the places we love
I'll show you what's in my head

Let's paint the moon
Let's paint your room
We'll paint your window
So light can shine through

Let's paint the clock
A quarter past noon
We'll paint that park
The one we always walk through

I'll mix it up
I don't care about the rules
When I am next to you
I will mix red and yellow if I want to
Nothing will stop us
From creating something new

We'll find a new color
One we'll call our own
We will paint it on our drawing
Of our future home
A place where we can be alone

Every scene we make
I'll hang in my room
So I can always remember you

Jersey Line

Heading down
This Jersey line
When we arrive
We'll stop at
The first bar we find
Raise our glasses
To the sky
Make new friends
Never say goodnight
When it's getting late
We'll slip away
Running up the street
Across the boulevard
Finding the sand
As we fall on the beach
I watch
As your hair flows back
The magic
From that ocean breeze

Green Eyes

Green eyes
   A perfect smile
A look making me
   Run a mile
Just to see you

Trips With You

I could lay here for hours
Out in the country
Far from everything
Under the night sky
As the wind brushes your hair
With so many stars above
But my eyes are only for you

I treasure these trips
These moments together
When time feels endless

The longer the distance

The better

Because with each stretching mile
Means another second with you

Friday Night

It's a Friday night
Just the two of us

Oh
I forgot

The rest of the crew

They're all around us
But all I can hear is you

It's Five O'Clock

It's five o'clock
Babe I'm in the parking lot
It's time to be who we are
Throw away everything we're not
The top's coming down
We're going to leave this town
My engines on
I'm ready for the long night
The door opens
Your face is looking bright
And you got on those shorts I like
Your favorite song's on the radio
You sing without a care in the world
I grip the wheel
Ready to take on this road

I know at the end
We'll need to have that long walk
I promise
We'll talk
For now
Sit back

Enjoy this moment
This is our one chance
Our last shot
To fall in love before it's gone
Our only chance
To make this real

The Perfect Date

We go out for dinner
Talk about family and where we're from
We hook arms
Stroll around the lake
It's getting late
We don't care time's ticking
The night takes us to a mini golf course
Next to your old high school
Which you didn't even know existed
Until this night
You're competitive
I like that
I beat you
What did you expect
Loser has to buy ice cream
You weren't getting off easy
I lay on the grass
Hands out for you to lift me up
But instead you fall next to me
Into my arms
Not caring who will see
We watch a storm from my car

In the abandoned parking lot
Kissing as lightning strikes far across the field
My car is off
It's getting hot
Sweat drips down my head
As I lean closer
You lean forward
I feel the heat from your mouth
We both never want to leave this moment
Because tomorrow
Life will drift us apart

Before We Say Goodbye

You give me a feeling I can't explain
When we sit in my car
In the abandoned parking lot
Watching the rain
Fall upon the windshield
As we talk for hours
About the dreams filling our minds
Forgetting everything going on in life

And I need to forget

Because tomorrow
We will have to say goodbye
As our dreams
Take us on two different roads
So let's enjoy what we have tonight
Before we say goodbye
Before we say goodnight
But let's not think about this just yet
Keep telling me more about your life

When You Leave My Car

You're stepping out of my car
But I pull you back into my arms
I can't let you go just yet
Because I don't ever want to forget
How it feels when you kiss me there
How it smells when my nose is in your hair
How it sounds when I make you laugh
It's going to hurt to see you go
After all these feelings have grown

We'll never know how this story will end

If I could have one superpower
I would stop us in this moment forever
So we will never see the sun
And tomorrow never comes

W o r d s   t o   a   G i r l

Hey
I had a lot of fun
Beating your butt at mini golf
And touching it too
I want to see you again
But
I don't want to keep asking
And make you feel pressured
To hang out with me
So I'm putting the soccer ball on your side
If you want to go out again
You let me know
And I'm all yours

It Hurts

It hurts to know
This is the last time
The last night
I'll see you like this
Because in a few days
You'll be gone
And I'll only be left
With your kiss

No Plan

When we were young
We were so in love
We'd ride our bikes
Until it was late
Take pictures
While making a funny face
We'd run on the beach
Fall together hand in hand
As our bodies became lost in the sand
It was back when we were young
When we had no plan

I ' m a M a n

If you want to be with me
Create another lane on that one-way street
Don't wait three days to text me
I know I'm a man
But I'm human too
I get nervous just like you
I may not show it
But I just want you to know
When you're safe in my arms
My heart's racing
Wondering
If I'll get more scars

High School Memory

Remember when we kissed
In front of every one
In the hall
During school
All those notes
I wrote only for you
The ones
I snuck
Inside your locker
While you were in class
Bored
Waiting for
The bell to ring
Have you kept them
After all these years

Until the Sunrise

Your face
Your eyes
You look so beautiful tonight
I don't know how
You get them to look so bright
I just want to gaze at them
Until the sun rises

And we'll sit on the beach until dawn
Talking about
Eveything that's going on
All your pain
All your suffering
All your joy
Matters so much to me
Every word from your mouth
Is a beautiful melody

History

When we were free
One second apart
Felt like an age
To my heart

When we were free
So many pages
Of history
I'll never change it

When we were free
Young and wild
And honestly
I'll never flip this page

Because when I do
Our story will become
History

No Summer Plans

I hate
Making plans for the summer
Because I hate
How fast it makes it go by
You meet someone new in the beginning
Before you know it
You're saying goodbye

This is why
I hate making plans for the summer

But here I am
Making plans
I'm making plans this summer

With you

Stage 2

Love

Our Fairy Tale

I always imagined
For us to end up like this
To fall in love with you
To have an ending with a kiss
Like all those fairy tales
We grew up watching
Like Jack and Sally
Underneath
A starry night
When the moon is bright
On Halloween

L o v e   I s ...

Warmth of your skin on top of mine
Your legs curled around me like a vine
Hold my hand beneath the stars
Let go of everything this night is ours

You and I
Embracing forever
Making things fair
Working together
When we laugh it off and joke around
When you stumble to the ground

Take my hand
Hold on to me
This is where I want to be
Next to you beneath the stars
I'll keep you safe inside my arms

Lay your head
Gently on mine
We'll cuddle all night until day time
Your eyes twinkle beneath the sun

Taking my heart for a run

The speed is abnormal
When I'm with you
I hope you know my love is true
All the times we have shared
There's more to come
So don't be scared

Warmth of your skin on top of mine
Your legs curled around me like a vine
Hold my hand beneath the stars
Let go of everything this night is ours

How Love Begins

Love starts
With one step forward
Watch your feet
Because one trip
Can ruin everything you did
Everything you worked on

Take one step
Two steps at most
Watch your fall
Make sure you get up
On your feet and breathe
Try again
Take it easy

Find your balance
Hold on to me
I will always be there
It's a guarantee to you
A promise
Which will never
Be broken

Find your way
I will guide you
Hold my hand
Never let go
Because the thoughts we share
Keep us together and going

To Hear My Love

Can you hold me tight and say it's true
Can you feel it's right
From what we've been through
Don't you know
I will be there
Every time you're scared

Don't you know
I will sing this song for you
From the bottom of my heart it's true
Every time you are alone
You will hear my love

The One

One star for every moment
We share beneath this moonlit sky
Underneath this endless night-time
One kiss to last forever
Light the night
Fly away to the stars above
Never bring me down
Never let me settle
Follow me
We'll find a new place
To discover
Mark it with the love we bring
Love that will last forever
Every moment we are together
Brings us closer than we ever thought was true
Hold me now

In Love

Your hair blows
In the light fall breeze
As we gaze up past the trees
To the sky above
I spread my body
So I feel free

The stars
They shine on us
As I lean over to kiss your lips
Taking me
Away from this world
Away from this place
Beyond outer space

A warm sensation
Of your skin against mine
As our legs fall in place and intertwine
I gaze into those eyes
I know that you're mine
The world brought us together
This is our line

The grass leaves our feet
As we become complete
Your eyes of stars bring me life
Filling every single one of my scars

A crescent moon shines
It takes the shape of a smile
Always looking down on us
To show us love and trust

Our lips touch and light
A spark brightening the night
In your eyes
I see mine
And I know
Our love will never die

Forever, Tonight

(Part One)

You had me at hello
But you made me work some more
I couldn't wait to explore
Everything about you

Love is not a choice
But a trigger by the heart
It's your turn to do your part
So go and set her off

Just say those words
And I will be there
I will be there
Forever

Follow me there
It will be all right
Just take my hand
Tonight, tonight

When you are lost
I will find you

Don't worry I'll come
Tonight, tonight

When times are rough
I'll hold you close
I'll tell you I'm there
Tonight, tonight

Just remember
I love you
I will be there
Forever, tonight

Forever, Tonight

(Part Two)

But times will be rough
We will fall down
We will rise again
Love will be found

Don't lose your hope
Don't lose your trust
Everything will work
It will work for us

Just say those words
And I will be there
I will be there
Forever

Follow me there
It will be all right
Just take my hand
Tonight, tonight

When you are lost
I will find you

Don't worry I'll come
Tonight, tonight

When times are rough
I'll hold you close
I'll tell you I'm there
Tonight, tonight

Just remember
That I love you
I will be there
Forever, tonight

I love you
Forever, tonight

Analogies on Love

Love
It's the core to an apple
You have to work hard
To get to the center
So you can reach those seeds
To make more grow

Love
It's like a clock
The big hand
Is the overall picture
And the little hand
Is all the fun in between

Love
It's like a wave
It will start off strong
All will crash down
But in the end
It will always come back

Love
It's like a mountain
A mountain I want to overcome
To get to the top
And yell out to the world
Every thing I feel

Love
It's like a piggy bank
It is never happy
Until its insides are full
With that feeling it knows
All too well

S h i e l d

Thunderous roars from the skies above
A little boy wrapped in a mother's love

A couple embraced in each other's arms
Protected from any cause of harm

A warrior scared from the sound of war
Seeks cover behind a metal board

Your favorite wind flows through your ears
Takes you away from the world, away from fear

A broken heart that slowly recovers
Builds up a wall from a former lover

Safe from the world inside your home
A place where you can be alone

An existence outside is only pondered
So we're stuck inside what we always wondered

Two arms coming back from another round
Keeping life in motion, but tightly bound

Blocked or protected by an object's meaning
One's entity is another's being

When the World Ends

Even if it is
The end of the world
You will still be my girl
I will never let you go
I will hold you
Before we die
Just breathe
Keep your hands in mine
We will move on
But our love will survive
Even if this is
The last time
I will ever look into your eyes
I will smile and tell you
You will always be mine

Leaving for College

We'll cruise this Jersey line
Leaving it all behind
Wherever we go
I want you to know
You will always be mine
We'll soon meet the divide
Where we'll need to decide
But wherever we go
I want you to know
You will always be mine
We'll meet that time in our lives
Where it all seems to fall out of line
If I don't make it home
I need you to go
Tell me everything will be all right
We'll look back to see where we've gone
As the years go by and everything moves on
If we don't make it home
I want you to know
I've had the time of my life

I'll Come Back

No matter how far time goes
I will never let you go
We will have to choose a road
Fall deep into the unknown
And yeah
Times will get rough
This road we're on will get tough
But I'll come back to you
And I know you'll come back too
I know you'll come back

Afternoons on Sunday

When I'm tired
I think about what's coming for me
At the end of this week
I know it's Thursday
But I look at my watch
To take another peek
It's nearly time to
Get away from this place
I know you're waiting
It's time to open up the gate

How much longer
Because I don't think I can make it
To the end of this week
It's almost over
I couldn't help it
I had to take a peek
It's nearly time to
Get away from this place
I know you're waiting
It's time to get this week erased

It's afternoons on Sunday
That have me feeling this way
When we lie in bed all day
Telling stories of our best days
Like when we passed the time in your room
When we were back in high school
And it's afternoons on Sunday
That have me feeling this way

And it's the times I like the most
When we lie in bed at home
Watching reruns of *Game of Thrones*
Wishing you were Khaleesi
And I was Jon Snow
I know this night will end
Time will start again
But next week is not too far
And we'll pick up where we are

A Simple Phone Call

I'm glad you called
I've been thinking about you
    All the time
It's nice to hear your voice
Even nicer
When it's here
    Mixed with mine

Appreciate Love

Appreciate the ones you got
  Appreciate the ones you had
   Love the ones you love
     The ones who love you back

About Life

Life is about being there
Making someone happy
So call them up
Tell them how you feel
Make their day
When it's their birthday
Travel those miles
Just to surprise them
Show up at their doorstep
Make them smile
Share your love
Share your life
Share your thoughts
Share your fights
Don't shake hands
Hug it out
Life's too short
To wish you had

Giving Love

Every girl I've dated
I've had second thoughts about
Is it something on my side
Something I'm not doing right
I try and try to give my love
But that doesn't seem to be enough
Because I always turn and walk away
When they offer their love to me

Except for you

You somehow broke down my wall
When the others
Couldn't even make it fall
To this day
I don't know what you did
The ones who pass by
They can't repeat it
You're the only one
Who has gotten by
How did you do it
When so many had tried

Stage 3

Disillusion

Scattered Mess

I look up now
To the sky above
To search your face
In the scattered mess

*First published by The Messenger Literary Magazine in October 2020.

The Way We Met

You were the girl
Who helped me with my life
Made me feel good about myself
You were the one
Who knew how to cheer me up

But where did that all go

I'm tired of all the fighting
Of all the yelling
It's all we do now
Can you see I'm overwhelmed
What ever happened
To that warming laugh
I know you're happy deep down inside
Just take a moment to remember

Remember the first time
We saw each other
Beautiful eyes
Hair
A perfect smile

You made me laugh
On the couch that night
When we watched *Forgetting Sarah Marshall*
In each other's arms
On my friend's couch
Do you remember it
The way we fell for each other
No hesitation
The way we connected
How happy we were
On that unforgettable night
Which brought us to this moment

I know two years went by fast
It's easy to forget
All we've been through
Take a second to breathe
Remember us
Because I can't imagine
This world without you

C o n f u s e d

Sitting in my room
I look out to the stars
All the poison in me
I try to disregard...

Ignorance conquered you
For what you are
I know the real you
Is trapped inside those bars
Because I never did
Quite understand
In the end
When you said
You wanted me
As a friend

You wanted things
Far better than myself
Why did it take me
All this time to see
I thought you were
Just scared and confused

But then again
That's all I wanted to assume

I never wanted it
To be this way
But nothing seems
To go my way
Screwed over seems
Like my middle name
When all I do
Is think of you
And you're out doing
Whatever it is
You do these days

You think I am okay inside
But my head is filled
With poison
It seeps through my veins
Even when I try
So damn hard
Not to think of you this way

I have no choice
But to wonder
In the end
Will you rely on me
To take you back

And clean up the dust

So tell me
What have all these years
Meant to you
Because I'm a mess
Torn up inside
As these clouds
Keep passing
Over my head

    But please
      Don't do a thing

    I will take care of the pain this time

You keep doing
What you're doing
I'll heal on my own
I'll become the man
Conquer the pain
And you will just
Stay the same

W a i t   f o r   M e

Wait for me
While I make this right
I'm sorry
For all the pain
We will get through it
Don't cry just yet
Please hold your tears
All waves crash
Returning stronger than before

I'm losing you
Lost touch
The spark went out
It's time to change
Make it new
Fix it now
I won't let us stumble
Into this hole
I won't wait to see
What we've created go
Wait for me

Wait for me
While I make this right
I'm sorry
For all the pain
Hold on tight to me
I won't let you fall
Follow me to the end of time

I'm sorry
For all the trouble I caused
Feel my pain
As I pull for you
I don't want to let go of this
I will use all my strength
To bring you back up

Lie on the couch
Be here next to me
Stare into my eyes
Tell me everything
You have my heart
Keep it safe from our enemy
Protect it from the stabbing pains
That can bring us harm

Hold me through the night
Don't you dare let go
Keep me safe

From everything
Warm my skin
Because I am so cold

Our wings are so small
But let's learn how to fly
A night won't do it
Give it some time
Let's make them stronger
So we can take to the sky
And soar real high

Just wait for me

What Happened to Us

We smiled
Like shy little kids
Ones who first fall in love
Your touch on my arm
How it made me feel
   So alive
Just seeing you
Made me feel
Different inside

But what has happened to those days

Where we loved each other
When we said we'd never let go
Now we fight
We never get along
I miss you like crazy
I need you home
All I want is for us
To be us again

D o n ' t G i v e U p

    Please
Don't shed your tears
There's still time
To save us
Our love is too strong
To end like this
So I promise you
    I will make all of this better

    Please
Don't toss it away
All your hope
Trust me like before
We can make this work
You don't need
To wash me away
Because I promise you
    I will make this better

    Please
Hold tight
Onto this sturdy rope

I will keep pulling you up
From your steep fall
I will pull and pull
And pull and pull
Because I promise you
I will not lose you forever
   So I will make this better

 Please
  Don't give up
   I will make us better

F l o w e r

I gave you a flower
A symbol of our love
But in the end I forgot
Flowers die

I N e e d Y o u

Hold me close tonight
I need your warmth
To know you're there
To see the light
I am scared of change
And what it has to bring
Will you be there for me tomorrow
Please look me in the eyes
I need to know the truth
Because as I go to bed tonight
I know

I only want you

After a Perfect Night

You said you'd be there in the morning
But you just left me lying alone this way
What happened in the past hours
Last night our love was stronger
Than any other night we had
Maybe I was caught up in the lights
Because you said this started before tonight
When you lost all your feelings for me
And now I'm stuck here believing
All the lies you left me here with
How can any of this be true after last night
The greatest time of my life

Broken Mirror

You are like
  A broken mirror

    There are so many reflections of you

  But I can't tell
Which one is true

All My Colors

Where did the colors go
Of my rainbow
All that's left is black and white
After you left our fight
Not even a few colorful shades
Against a gray sky
After you said goodbye

J e j u n e

I fall to the ground
Every time I see you here
Without the smile
You used to bring

Yes
My feelings once
Were so naive

But I swear
I've grown
So please
I beg you
Don't fade away

Into Your Arms

As I lie outside
I begin to realize

I am not who I am supposed to be

The moon is so far
I go to grab it
But miss
Falling back into your arms

Back to where I started

The Last Song

You're like the first song on the album
Full of power and popularity
To catch your attention right away
Without the real sound or right emotions
To steal your heart

I'm like the last song
With emotion and meaning
Making you work for the end
Because it's about the journey
All the turns and the bends
Suffering
Pain
And hard times
All which help you
Grow

Don't Forget Me

When the shores are gone
Just look for the stars
And don't forget me
Don't forget me

When the winds are strong
Listen for my song
And don't forget me
Don't forget me

Don't cry as I sail away
I'll come back for you some day

Under Your Feet

Go out in the world
Search for my heart
Where we first met
Is where you should start
When I looked at you
You smiled at me
The magic between us
We couldn't believe it

Go out in the world
Search for my heart
I'll give you a hint
Where you should start
Go out by the sea
So you can finally see
I buried it
Under your feet

Love Pulls Through

Don't go
Don't leave
You know it's me
You need to stop

Believe

Don't fight
Don't cry
It's all right to try
Take a moment

Breathe

I'll wait
I'll try
To undo this goodbye
The sky will fall
But love pulls through it all

The years
We shared

I fear despaired
I feel you falling away
Grab on
Hold tight
I'm strong tonight
I won't let you slip away

I'll wait
I'll try
To undo this goodbye
The sky will fall
But love pulls through it all

Waiting for War

As I wait outside
The rain begins to wash my face
It takes away the pain
As we wait to go to war
I wonder
If I bleed
Will I survive
Will I make it through the night
Can I shed
A little blood
Just to win your love
I am here
Side by side
With others fighting
For love
The horns blow
We march forward
And I wonder
Will I live
To see you with me again

I Can Make It Better

I like sharing my heart
Expressing my mind
You're the only one who listens
Time after time
When I fall down
You bring me to my feet
You'll work for that smile
You never admit defeat

That's why
I can't find a reason
This is all gone
Why are you leaving
What did I do wrong
I can fix it
I can send you more letters
So why do you admit
We'll never get better

The Queen

I wake up every morning
Thinking this will be the day
When everything will be okay
But when I get up
You already found
A way inside my head
You have me on my knees
  Begging

Because you're the queen
Who conquered me

You contain the power
To set me free

Picture Frame

That picture frame
The one which holds
So many memories
Sits underneath
The wall covered in
Pictures of you and me

But lately
Everything has been
A little bit hazy
All the colors seem
To be fading away
And lately
Things have been
A little bit crazy
All the colors
Of the photo
Are turning gray

Wrong Side of the Road

I'm on the wrong side of the road
Where the line isn't broken
I'll go until it breaks
I'll drive until it opens

I see you over there
Driving from the truth
You're on the side that is free
But I can't come over to you

I will drive until it opens
I will drive to get to you
Every road has its ending
So you can drive somewhere new

And I will never give up
I will drive to make this be
There's one thing I'm certain
You were meant for me

I Want the Truth

What happened to me
  What happened to you
    What happened to everything that was us

    Who is he

    I want the truth
   Because I thought we were
So madly in love

A Dream

Little did I know
I was following a dream
Just like everyone
In front of me

I thought
I could go and see
What love truly is
What love really means

But little did I know
Everyone else
Was going for
The same exact dream

Senior Year

It was my senior year
Instead of seeing friends
I gave you my hand
I loved you so much
I guess you didn't understand
After those next few months
I knew I'd be seeing you
But saying goodbye to them
It didn't mean I wasn't devoted
Or didn't care about you
I just thought you'd understand
I needed some time with friends

Not into This

Another phone on the table
I laugh
Check another off the list

So I try again

But I guess manners aren't in style
Because I try again and again
And never get a thank you
After buying drinks

I'm pissed
And I laugh
When I get the text
Saying you're not into this

After Only a Date

We went on one date
And I thought it went great
We were laughing all night
I got the feeling something might
Go a little further
But I never heard from you
After only a date

It doesn't mean
I want to marry you
If I ask you to go to the zoo
I just thought it would be cute
And it's something nice to do
But I scared another away
After only a date

It doesn't mean
I want to get down on one knee
Did I mention going to the zoo
Is completely free
I would go by myself
But I thought I'd give you a chance

However
I scared another away
After only a date

It doesn't mean
I want to amalgamate
If I ask you to ice skate
I just thought the weather was nice
And it might be fun
But I scared another away
After only a date

You can't learn
About someone's heart
If you don't give it
A chance to spark
One date isn't enough
It's like they think
I'm already planning
I want three sons
Jake
Steven
And little Johnny Run
But I scared another away
After only a date

Little did they know
A second call

Was never in my plans
But I thought I would give them
Another chance
After only a date

Enough Friends

I can't bare to hear it again
That you only want to be friends
It's too late in the game
I have enough of them

I know it may be selfish

But

If you will not take me in the start
I will not see you in the end

If We Didn't Have It

What would it be like
If we didn't have it
Would I get to hear your voice
Would I be focused more on the present
Or still stuck in a void

What would it be like
If we didn't have it
Would we be a bit more honest
Instead of posting all these false images
Acting like it's the truth

Forgot Love

Love
How could we forget love
When we were so caught up in us

Truth
How could we forget truth
When we were so caught up in lust

We conquered mountains
We fought through walls
But we forgot it all
To die and fall

Like I Don't Exist

I hate
When you look at me
With those loving eyes
Reminding me
How much I love you

But then he walks in

Your head spins
Forgetting I exist

Now I stand here alone
Watching you two talk
Your skin inches closer
Than ours ever did

Your lips are on his

And I see so clearly
You love him

Counting Days

We used to count the days
How many more until I see you
But now when I count to ten
You're not here again
The numbers blew away
Caught in the wind
Sailing away

Perfect Cloud

And as I look up now
I see a perfect cloud

One that looks like us
I watch it drift apart

Recurring nightmares. Painful scars. Heartbreaking betrayals. A breakup can feel even more painful than losing a loved one. But the perfect way to overcome this insufferable stage is by connecting with poetry. Read *Stages of a Breakup* now!

Available now on Amazon!

For more information on *A Broken Heart Poetry Collection*, visit: **www.patrickjohnswrites.com/brokenheartpoetry**

Note From the Author: Thank you so much for reading! The support means the world to me. You can help other hopeless romantics find this poetry collection by leaving a review on Amazon and Goodreads! Every review matters!

Want to connect with more breakup poetry? Claim your copy of the bonus poetry chapbook *I Trusted You With My Heart* by signing up for Patrick Johns's newsletter:

https://subscribepage.io/poetrynewsletter

Born and raised in Ramsey, New Jersey, Patrick Johns attended university at Virginia Tech, obtaining degrees in engineering and mathematics. Go Hokies!

However, writing is Patrick's true passion. After writing his first novel, *Junkland*, the first book in *The Hoarding* series, Patrick left his engineering job to teach English in Spain.

Four years later, Patrick returned to his roots to connect and spread his joy for books with readers all over New Jersey. When he's not writing, you can find Patrick surfing, hiking, traveling, or writing music.

To see what Patrick is up to, follow him on social media:

Instagram - @patrickjohnswrites
TikTok - @patrickjohnswrites
Facebook - @patrickjohnswrites
Twitter - @patjohnswrites

For more information about the author, visit his website:

www.patrickjohnswrites.com

Books by Patrick Johns

Fiction

The Hoarding

Junkland

The Lost Soul

Poetry

A Broken Heart Poetry Collection

Stages of a Scattered Mess

Stages of a Breakup

Made in United States
Troutdale, OR
03/29/2024

18663883R00076